For those trying to come out of the closet of paralysis ...
Whether your closet is one of fear of speaking up for what you
know to be right,
Whether it is one of an inability to act on your convictions, or
Whether it is one of knowing you made the wrong and irrevocable
decision ...
Forgive yourself and act.

The Intactivists
San Francisco Pride 2009-2010

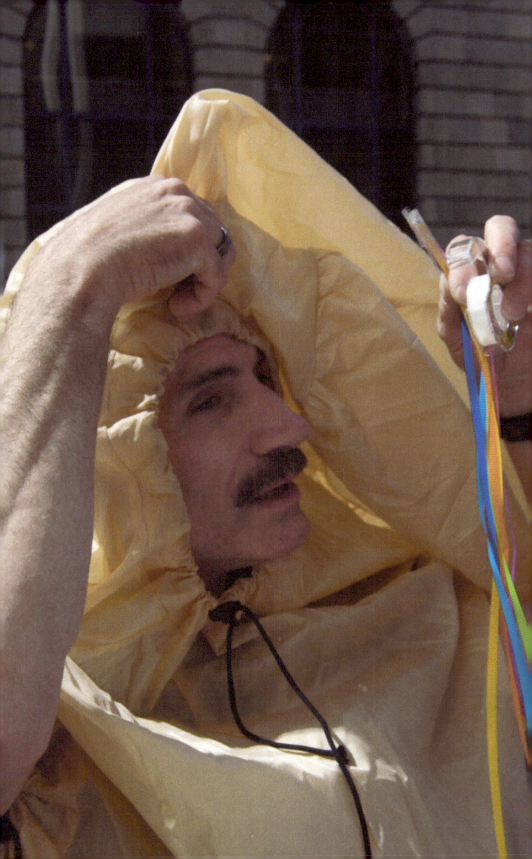

The Intactivists
San Francisco Pride 2009

An intactivist is a person who supports the fundamental human right of all people to intact genitals. While no gender or person is excluded from those intactivists seek to protect through lobbying and political action, infant boys are the most wide-spread victims of genital cutting in the United States. This book documents a very public manifestation of the intactivists of the the San Francisco Bay Area.

The first contingent of San Francisco Bay Area intactivists to march in the San Francisco Pride Parade did so in 2004 under the banner of the Bay Area NOCIRC Group. In 2005, the group returned under the banner of the Bay Area iNtactivists Group (BANG). From 2006, the group has been sponsored by MGMBill.org. In 2007, the group hosted a booth at the Pride Festival instead of marching in the Pride Parade. Otherwise, the group has become a regular feature in San Francisco's Pride Parade. This book documents the years 2009 and 2010.

I became involved with the group in 2006 and took it upon myself to document the by-now annual event starting in 2009. I owe a debt of gratitude to all the marchers and James Loewen, a long time Canadian intactivist, photographer and videographer, who has helped me with encouragement and pointers in the art of the photog.

- David Wilton

January 2, 2011

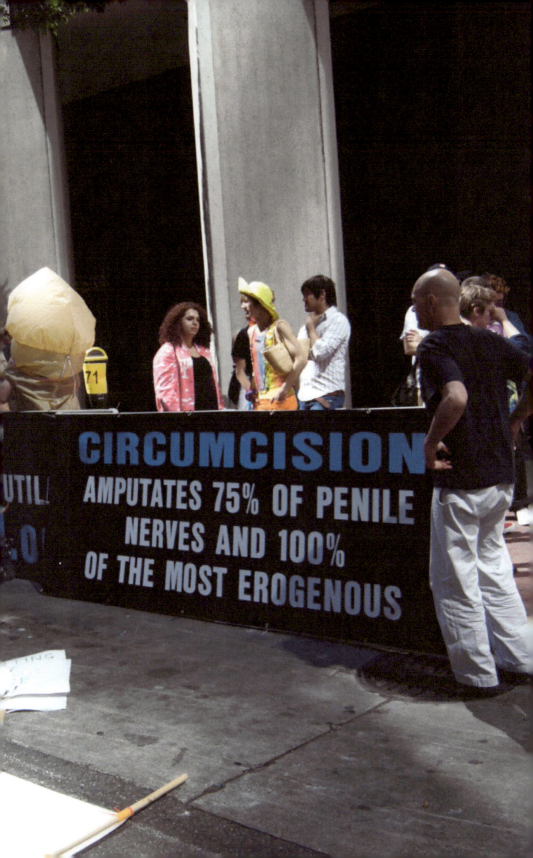

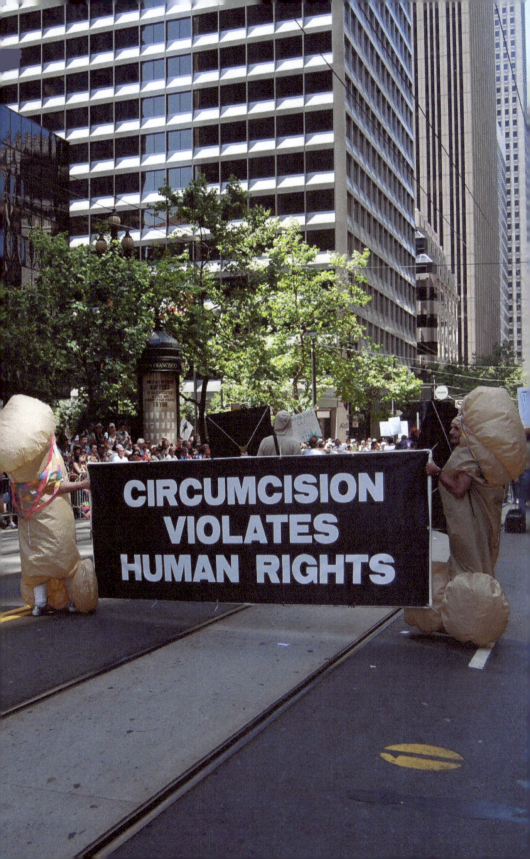

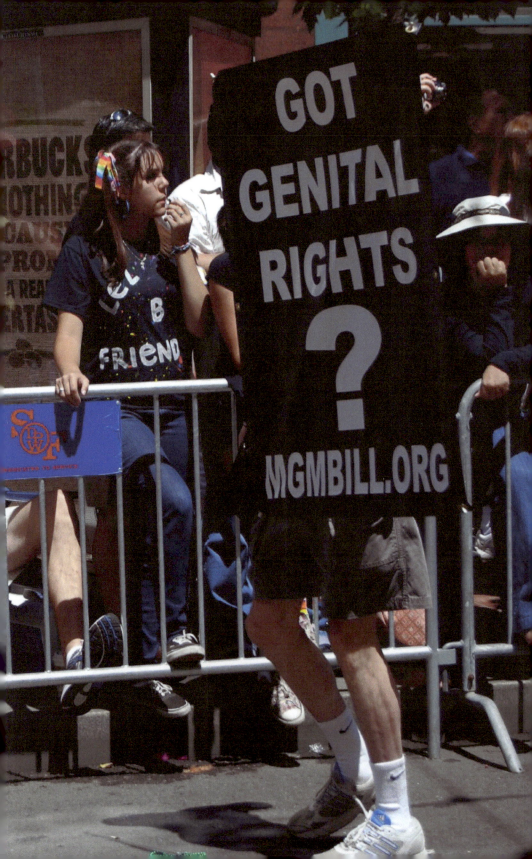

The Penis Costumes

The penis costumes came about as a way to engage the spectators directly when hopes of garnering media attention repeatedly failed. Year after year, coverage of the Pride Parade showered attention on half-naked dancers, men engaged in deep tongue kissing, and Dykes on Bikes, but no intactivists or intactivist signs or banners.

The response that the intactivist contingent came up with was to don penis costumes for the first time in 2008 and engage the spectators directly and leave the couch potatoes at home to their PG-rated version of the parade. At first, several marchers objected because the costumes looked circumcised. Several people found the costumes impossible to walk in. One of our group overheated both years they were used. The costumes were retired the following year.

CIRCUM

AMPUTATES 7

NERVES

OF THE MOST

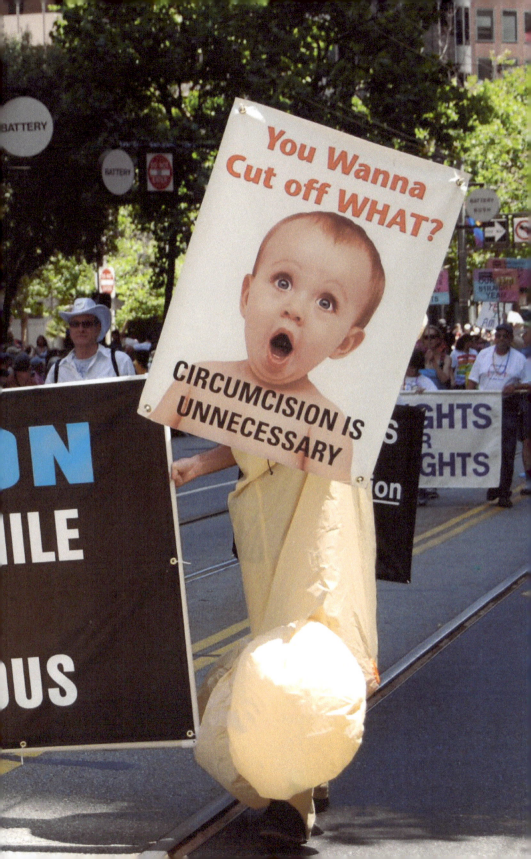

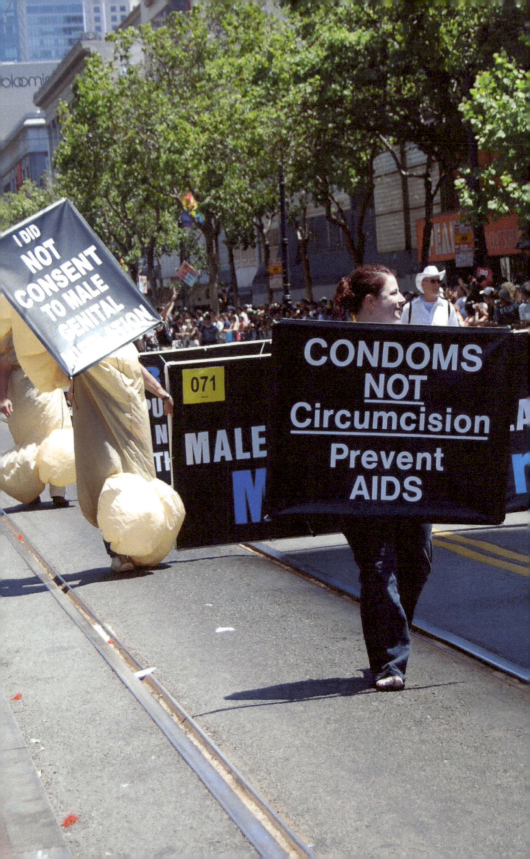

The Intactivist in the Steely Brassiere

The transexual in the steely brassiere was not planned. She jumped the barricades, as it were, and commandeered a sign from a member of the group. She made a greater impression than any penis costume could ever do.

There wasn't a half-hearted smile in the intactivists contingent. Many of us wondered if we had achieved a breakthrough. Finally someone with the power to make a showy impression had seen our message and been moved to act in an instant. Later many of us concluded that she wasn't entirely certain of our entire message. Later conversations proved she got the condoms part, but wasn't too clear on the anti-circumcision message.

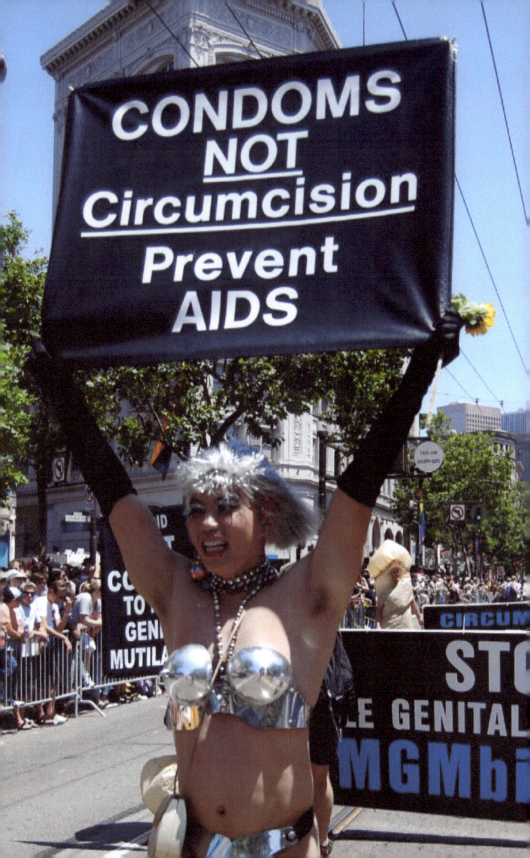

The Intactivists
San Francisco Pride 2010

In 2010, the penis costumes were retired in favor of new signs and new faces. We had a solid turn out. The Pride Parade theme of "Forty and Fabulous" in honor of the 40th year of the Pride Parade in San Francisco inspired our new positive message plastered across our new lead banner, "Foreskins are Fabulous." The message meshed nicely with the alliterative "Forty" being replaced with an almost equally alliterative "Foreskins."

The group seemed more cheerful and optimistic for 2010. By now, the shock of a resurgent circumcision lobby and the false hope and hysteria over HIV/AIDS as the new raison d'etre for pushing infant circumcision had worn off. Many were feeling more energized than ever. Our numbers may have been swelled by the ability of new tools to find each other. Facebook and Twitter came into their own over the previous 12 months and provided an outlet and a place to speak to an ever larger audience.

While there were no steely brassierred transexuals to make a splash in 2010, we had enough people to hand out cards with our message to spectators along the route. Personal and upclose engagement with onlookers felt like progress.

Foreskins

Fabul

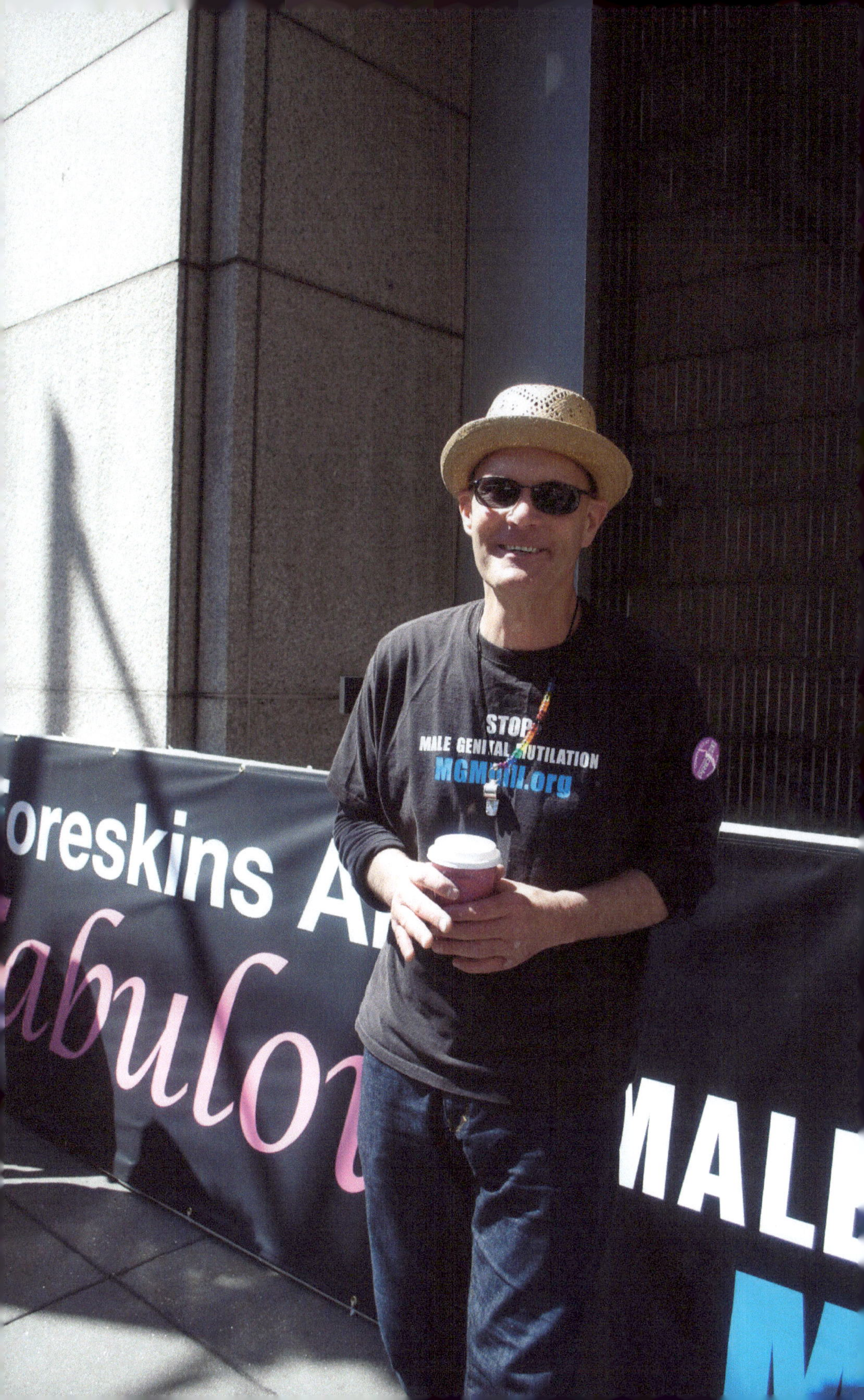
STOP
MALE

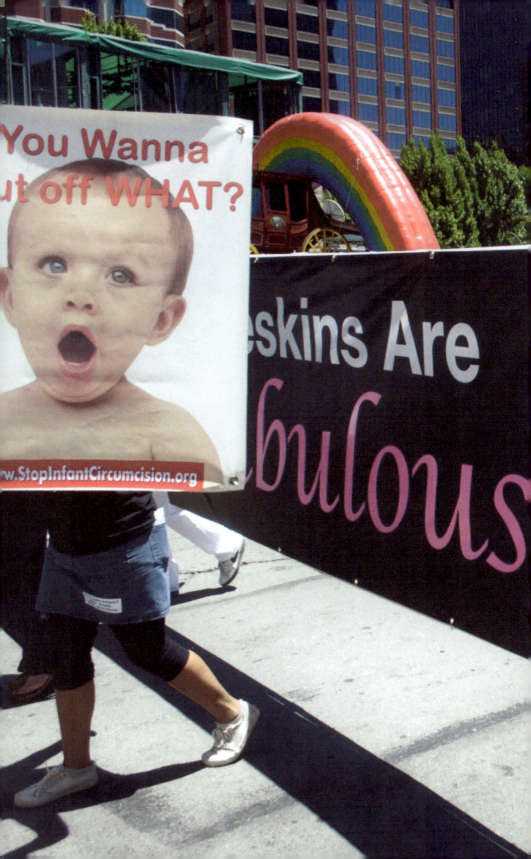

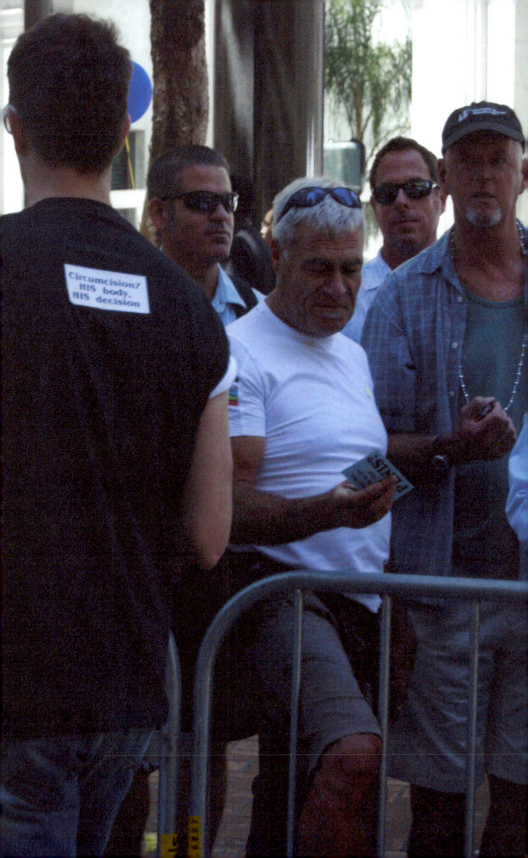

I DID
NOT
CONSENT
TO MALE
10 out of 10
BABIES
OPPOSE
CONDOMS
NOT
Circumcision
Prevent
AIDS
Take Your Whole
Baby Home
CIRCUMCISING
IS UNNECESSARY

Behind and In Front: Lawn Mowing Goats and Asexuals
Our Marching Neighbors

Every year our contingent gets marching neighbors. For 2010, we got the lawn mowing goats behind us. These gentle animals are rented out as a sort of green lawn mowing service. We were thankful they were behind us and not in front although they did ride in the back of a truck. In front of us were the equally gentle asexuals.

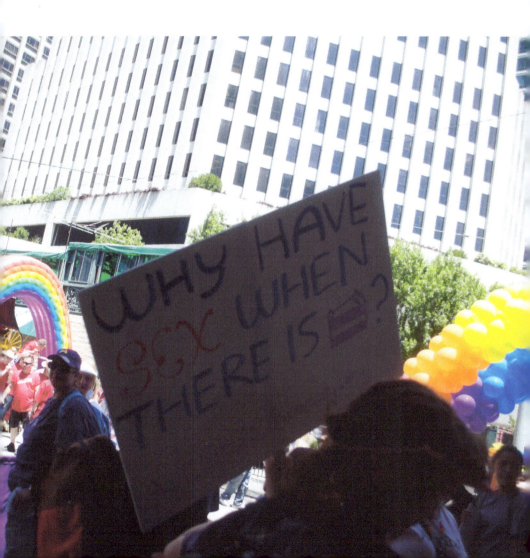

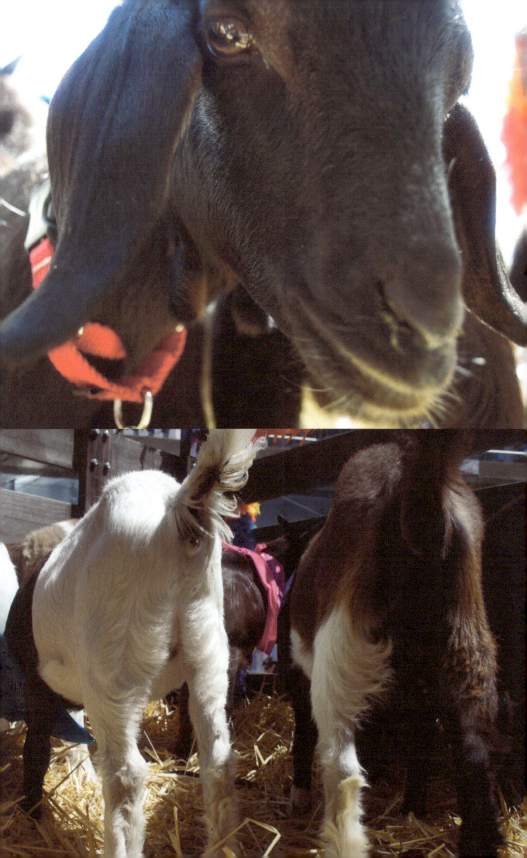

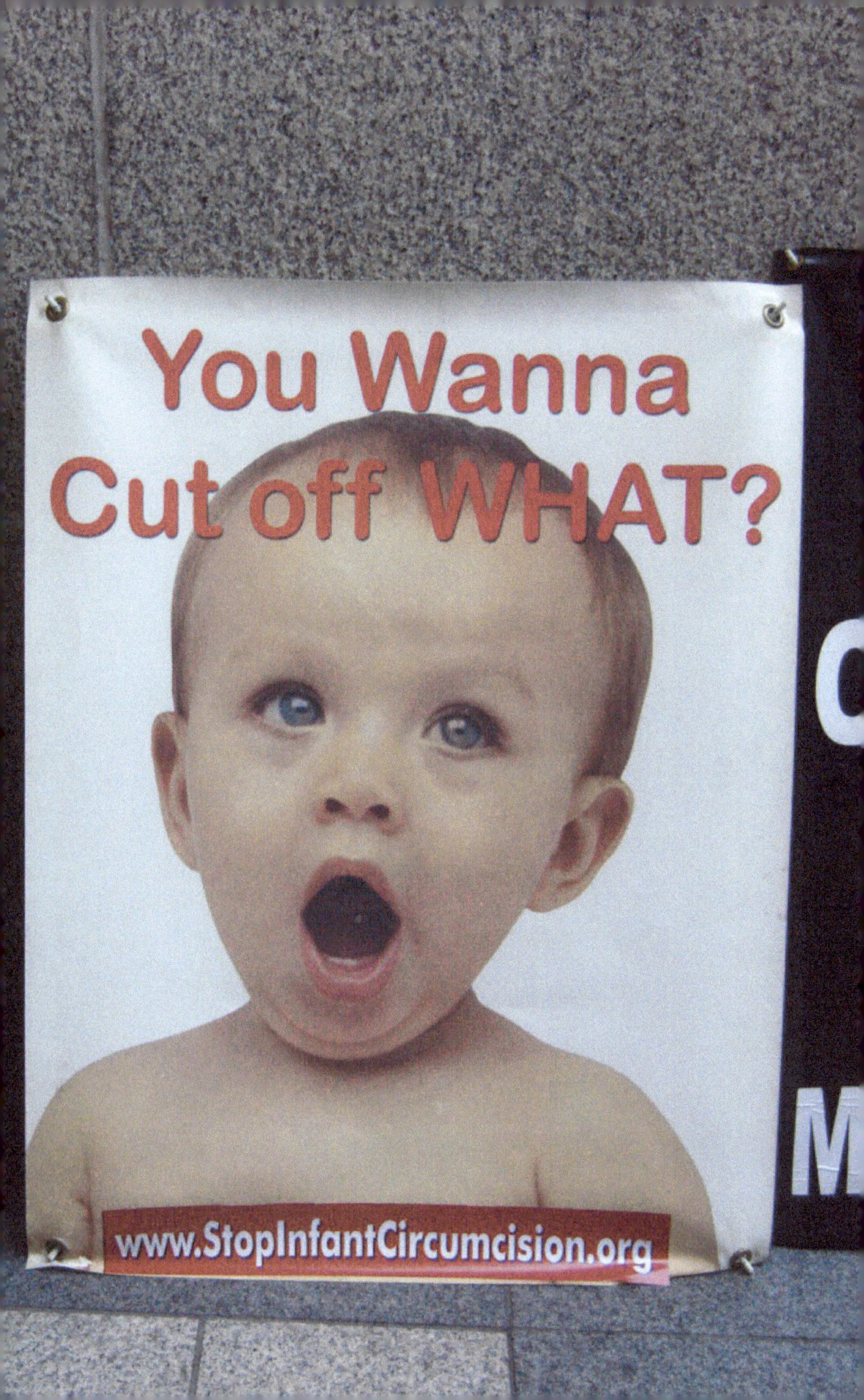
You Wanna
Cut off WHAT?
www.StopInfantCircumcision.org

Special thanks to:

All the members of the Bay Area Intactivists Group
Matthew Hess of MGMBill.org

Images and text by David Wilton

Published by MC_HIV
Copyright 2011

ISBN-13: 978-1456494582
ISBN-10: 1456494589

Please direct all inquiries to:

David Wilton
PO Box 40312
San Francisco, CA 94140
USA

david@davidwilton.net
http://www.circumcisionandhiv.com/

US$19.00

All proceeds from the sale of this book go to
support MC_HIV and related educational efforts.

www.ingramcontent.com/pod-product-compliance
Lightning Source LLC
Chambersburg PA
CBHW041144050326
40689CB00001B/484